FIRST REPERTOIRE
for LITTLE PIANISTS

BOOK 2

by Melanie Spanswick

Cover illustration by Laura Benavente

ISBN: 978-1-70515-473-1

WILLIS MUSIC

EXCLUSIVELY DISTRIBUTED BY

Copyright © 2022 by The Willis Music Co.
International Copyright Secured All Rights Reserved

Visit Hal Leonard Online at
www.halleonard.com

Contact us:
Hal Leonard
7777 West Bluemound Road
Milwaukee, WI 53213
Email: info@halleonard.com

In Europe, contact:
Hal Leonard Europe Limited
42 Wigmore Street
Marylebone, London, W1U 2RY
Email: info@halleonardeurope.com

In Australia, contact:
Hal Leonard Australia Pty. Ltd.
4 Lentara Court
Cheltenham, Victoria, 3192 Australia
Email: info@halleonard.com.au

PREFACE

ORIGINAL REPERTOIRE

First Repertoire for Little Pianists is a repertoire series for children from beginner to early elementary level. Each book contains a collection of 25 original piano pieces, including a selection of solo works (some with teacher accompaniment) and concert duets to be played with either a teacher or fellow student.

BOOK 2

"Book 2" consists of very short compositions up to 17 measures in length, which may be used alongside various piano method books or as performance pieces. The journey begins using separate hands, gradually combining both hands together.

FIVE-FINGER POSITIONS

In "Book 2," pieces begin to move out of the five-finger hand position of "Book 1." However, all five fingers are called to be employed optimally, boding well for future development. Accompanying performance notes are included alongside each piece. These are intended to help facilitate interpretation, note learning, and rhythmic literacy.

NOTE AND RHYTHMIC LEARNING

Understanding of rhythm is fundamental in the early stages of musical learning. This book focuses on whole, dotted half, half, dotted quarter, quarter, and eighth-note time values, and employs the following time signatures: 2/4, 3/4, and 4/4. Key signatures are limited to C, G, and F major, and A, E, and D minor, with the addition of some more tonally adventurous pieces.

DEVELOPING MUSICIANSHIP

Dynamics, phrase markings, tempo markings, fingering, and pedaling (where appropriate) are present throughout. There is also a selection of rote pieces along the way, to encourage movement around the keyboard.

HAVING FUN

There are also fun illustrations interspersed throughout this book, designed to fuel the imagination. Coloring these in will be an engaging activity, helping to facilitate further investment in the learning process.

Melanie Spanswick

CONTENTS

OUT OF THE BLUE

SOLO WITH TEACHER ACCOMPANIMENT

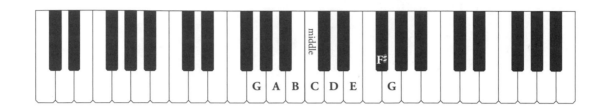

Bright and Bold

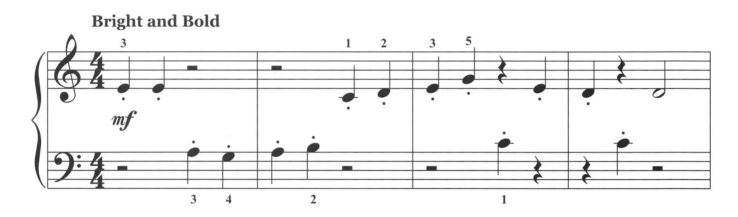

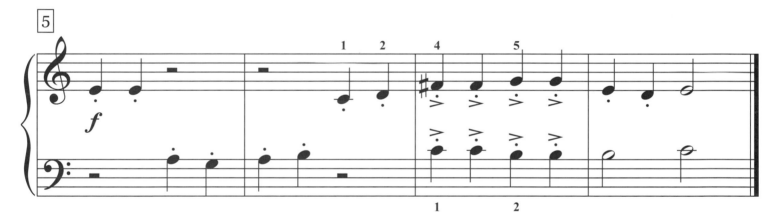

ACCOMPANIMENT

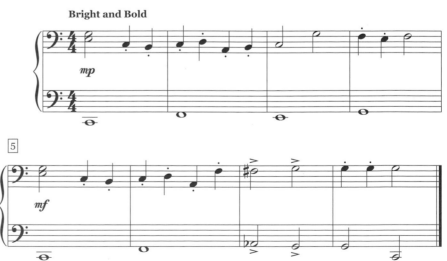

PERFORMANCE NOTES

Welcome to your first piece of *First Repertoire for Little Pianists: Book 2*. "Out of the Blue" refers to something unexpected. There are certainly some musical surprises in this piece, so watch out!

RHYTHM FOCUS

Rhythm refers to the patterns of long and short notes in music. Let's try tapping out the rhythm of the piece. It has four counts per bar. First, tap your right hand on the piano lid or your knee as if you are a ticking clock: steady and regular. Now do it again and count "1, 2, 3, 4" as you tap.

To tap the whole rhythm of "Out of the Blue," you'll need both hands. Be sure to use the right hand to tap the note values in the treble clef and the left hand for those in the bass clef. Here, the crossed noteheads show that there is no pitch.

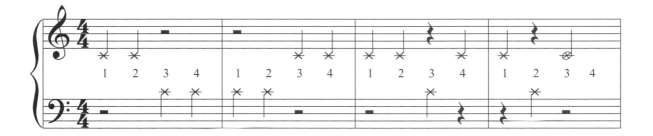

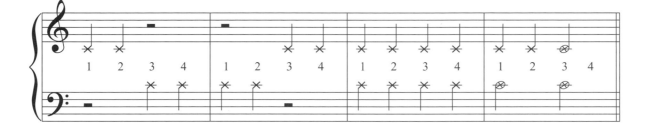

NOTE FOCUS

The quarter notes have dots underneath or above the noteheads. These show that we should play with a short, *staccato* touch. Practice the first measure and imagine the notes as raindrops, bouncing off a windowsill. When you bounce off each note, you will achieve a short, staccato sound. Some of the notes have an accent mark. An accent mark looks like this: ➤. Notes with this sideways arrow should be played with a heavier touch.

You might like to practice writing out the notes to help you learn them. Find the different notes used in this piece and write them out once on the grand staff below as noteheads without a stem. Then, write the letter names underneath. The first one has been done for you.

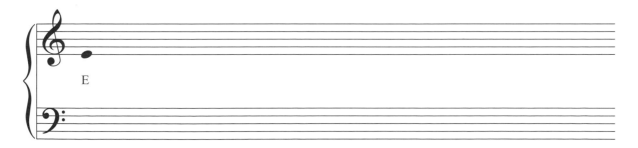

MIND THE GAP

SOLO

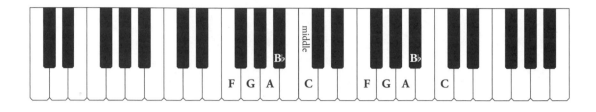

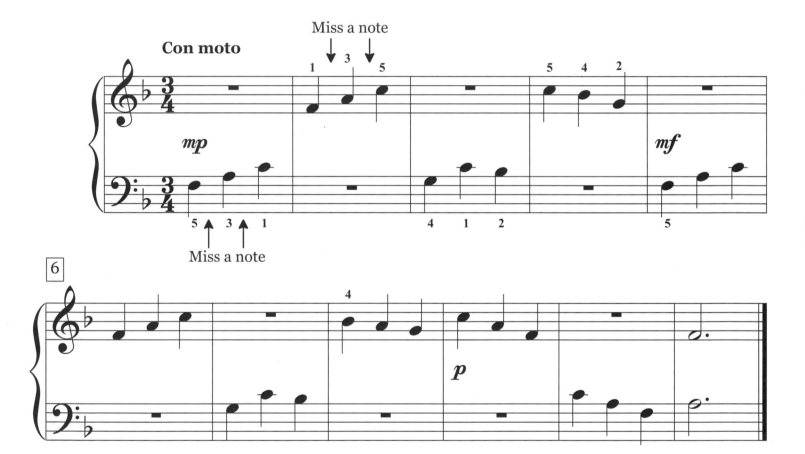

PERFORMANCE NOTES

The title of this piece comes from the fact that there are lots of spaces between the notes. Be sure to practice slowly and carefully so that you don't fall between the gaps!

RHYTHM FOCUS

Tap the rhythm of the music, saying the beat count as you go ("1, 2, 3"). Be sure to use the right hand to tap the note values in the treble clef and the left hand for those in the bass clef. Keep practicing until you are secure and confident.

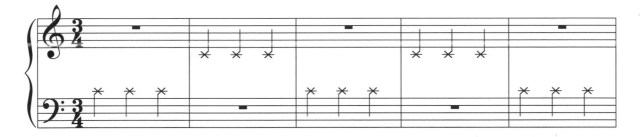

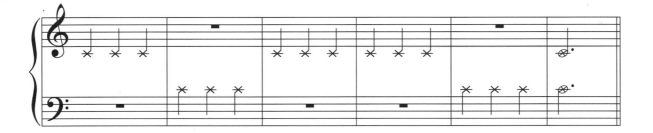

NOTE FOCUS

Each note in this piece must have a lovely, smooth touch. There should be no break in sound from one note to the next. You will find that each hand stays in a five-finger position throughout, so keep your fingers hovering close to the keys.

In this piece, not all of the notes you play are next to each other. There are lots of gaps in between them. The notes F, A, and C in measures 1 and 2 make up what is called a *broken chord*. If you play these notes at the same time, the chord is no longer broken! Playing them together forms a *chord*. To practice these measures, it can help to play the notes as chords, using the fingering below.

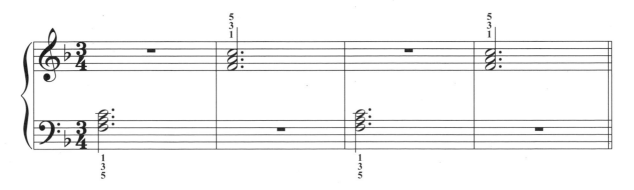

B♭ AND BE HAPPY

SOLO

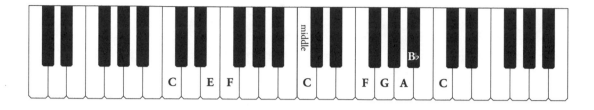

Moving Along

PERFORMANCE NOTES

This piece is full of lovely B♭s. Check the keyboard diagram at the top of the piece to be sure which black key this note lies on.

RHYTHM FOCUS

The left-hand part consists of just one whole note per bar. Play through the left-hand part on its own, counting four quarter-note beats per bar. Now, do the same while your teacher plays the right-hand melody.

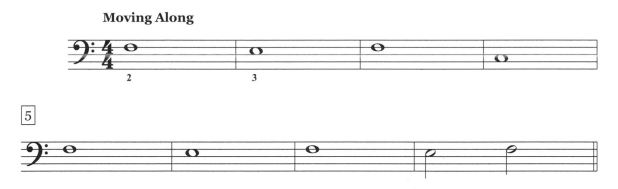

NOTE FOCUS

The right-hand part plays the tune or melody. Play each quarter-note beat firmly with a steady pulse. Try playing the right-hand part on its own. Finally, put both hands together and don't forget to add the dynamics. (The right-hand melody should be brighter than the whole notes in the left hand.)

GRUMPY FAIRY

SOLO WITH TEACHER ACCOMPANIMENT

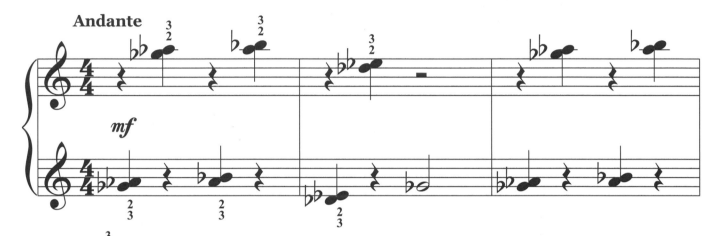

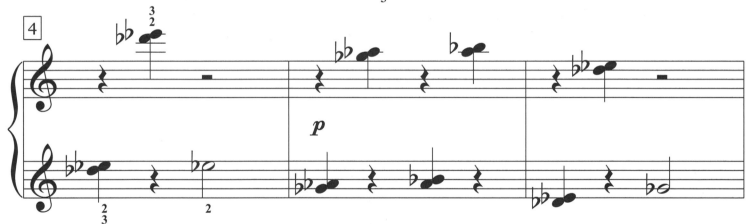

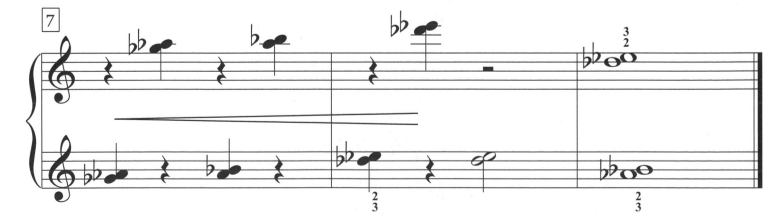

PERFORMANCE NOTES

"Grumpy Fairy" uses only black keys in note patterns that mainly involve finger numbers 2 and 3. This gives the piece a "grumpy" sound.

NOTE FOCUS

This piece is to be played by rote. This means that your teacher will show you the notes to play and you will memorize the note patterns. Enjoy performing this piece without needing to use the music and be sure to move around the keyboard quite quickly in order to play each note pattern in time. You can even ask your teacher to use the sustaining pedal throughout for a wonderful, hazy sound.

Both hands play in the treble clef for this piece. Can you draw a treble clef? Have a go at writing a few on the staff below.

ACCOMPANIMENT

MUDDY PUDDLES

SOLO

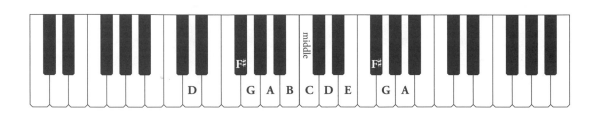

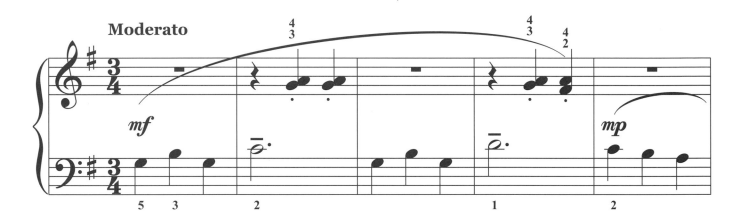

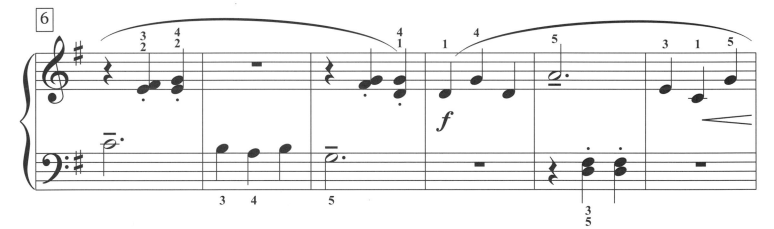

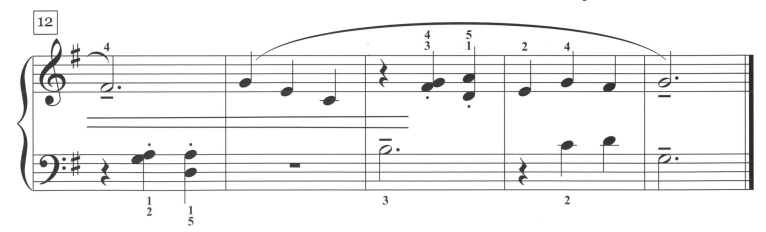

PERFORMANCE NOTES

Everyone loves jumping up and down in muddy puddles! But don't forget your boots…

RHYTHM FOCUS

This piece has three quarter-note beats per bar. Tap the rhythm on your knee or the piano lid using both hands. Keep the beat count going in your head ("1, 2, 3").

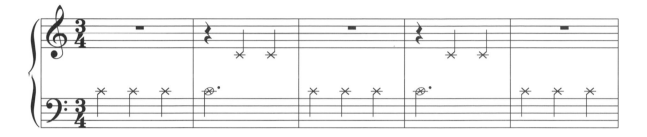

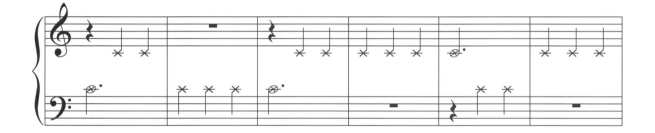

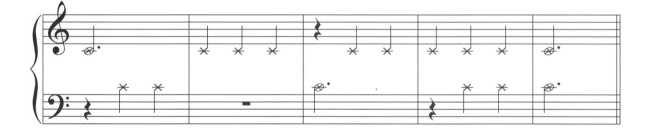

NOTE FOCUS

Every time you see the note F in this piece, you are actually going to play the F-sharp black key. The ♯ on the F line at the beginning of the piece tells us this. When playing black keys, your fingers will need to move a bit further "into" the keyboard, for firm placement. This is because the black keys are thinner than the white keys.

The left hand plays the tune during the first eight measures, so try to make sure you play it with a rich, warm sound. Practice hands separately to get this just right!

LONELY BILLY GOAT

SOLO

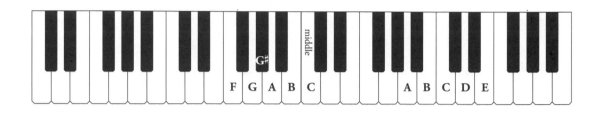

PERFORMANCE NOTES

Our little goat is all alone without any friends. The character of this piece shows how sad he is. Try and imagine this as you are playing.

RHYTHM FOCUS

If you've played all the pieces up to this point, you will have now performed the following note values: quarter note, half note, dotted half note, and whole note. Before we move on, review with your teacher the count for each note value, using the guide below.

QUARTER NOTE

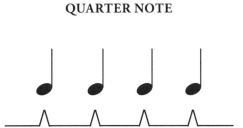

HALF NOTE

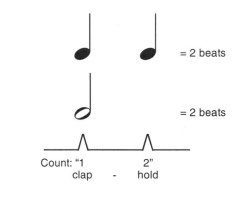

DOTTED HALF NOTE

WHOLE NOTE

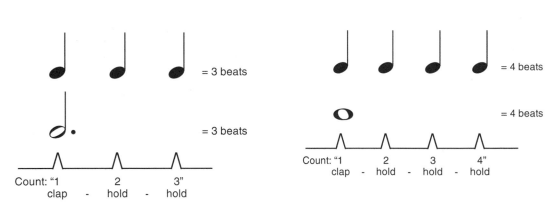

NOTE FOCUS

This piece has no sharps or flats in the key signature but there is a G♯ used in the music. Play a five-finger A minor scale, which will be a useful warm up for playing this piece.

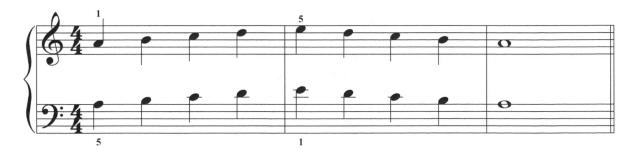

A FRIGHT IN THE NIGHT

SOLO WITH TEACHER ACCOMPANIMENT

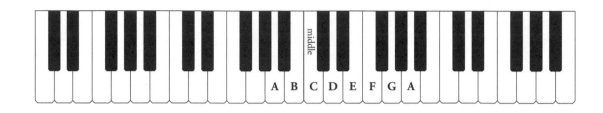

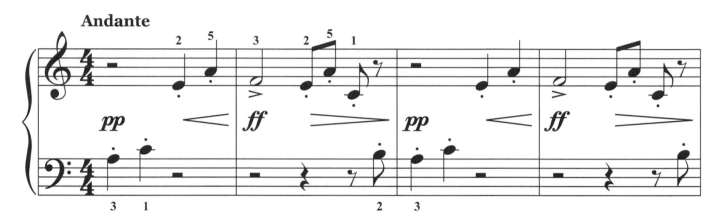

PERFORMANCE NOTES

This is a great piece to play for a Halloween concert. But beware, it has lots of spooky chords!

RHYTHM FOCUS

There are many eighth notes in this piece and it will be important not to rush them. One eighth note is half the value of a quarter note. To count eighth notes accurately, our beat count should be "1–and–2–and–3–and–4–and." Tap this rhythm out using both hands and say the beat count so that you are secure.

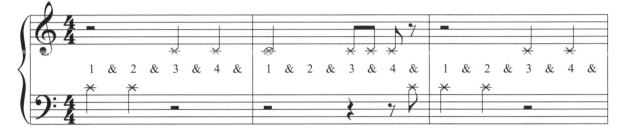

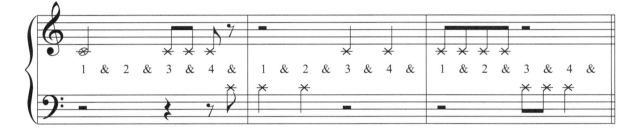

NOTE FOCUS

You may like to practice the right- and left-hand exchanges slowly. To really bring out the spooky character of this music, your accents and dynamics must be powerful and extreme.

ACCOMPANIMENT

CATCH ME IF YOU CAN

DUET

PERFORMANCE NOTES

This is the first duet in this book for you and a friend to play. You'll be chasing each other all over the keyboard in this fun piece!

RHYTHM FOCUS

Tap the rhythm with your duet partner and say the beat count out loud: "1–and–2–and–3–and–4–and." Make sure you tap exactly together; this is so important in duet playing. Counting eighth notes in the beat count as shown above will help with this. Here's a simple tapping exercise you can practice together. Say the beat count and make sure you are tapping in time. You can try the exercise at different speeds to test yourselves.

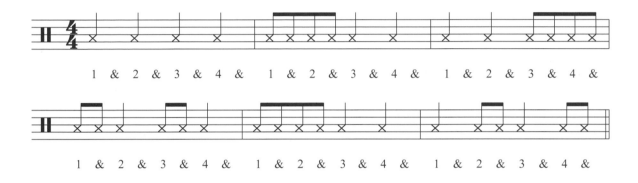

NOTE FOCUS

The dynamics of this piece are very important, too. Try an extension of the tapping exercise by including dynamics. Then, apply dynamics to your tapping of the piece itself. Once you can tap the piece perfectly in time, together, and with great dynamics, you know you'll be ready to add in the notes.

AS SWEET AS HONEY

SOLO

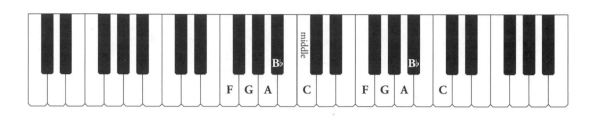

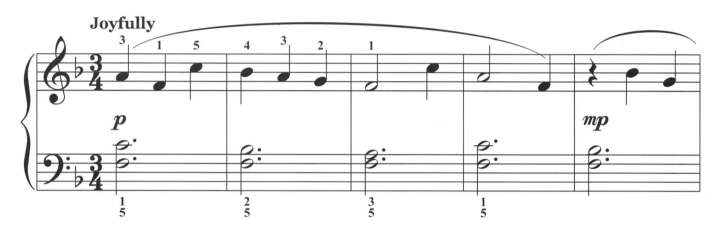

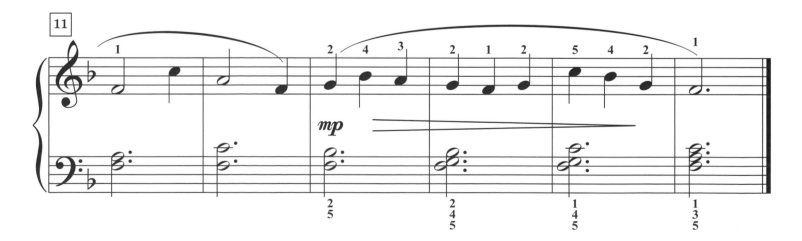

PERFORMANCE NOTES

This pretty piece is as sweet as honey. And with left-hand chords, there's plenty to work on to make sure you don't get stuck!

RHYTHM FOCUS

Let's play tic-tac-toe! Ask your teacher to play with you using quarter notes (the 0s), and you can play using half notes (the Xs). Place the half notes in a row of three before your teacher places their quarter notes and you have won the game! To help, a half note has already been added.

NOTE FOCUS

This left-hand part consists of chords (where we play two or more notes together at the same time). The lower note is always F, so aim to focus on changing the upper note. (Be sure to play every chord exactly together by depressing all notes at the same moment.)

The right-hand part will need a bright, bold sound, so encourage the fingers to play on their tips, fully pressing into the keys.

Practice hands separately to get both of these elements just right. It's helpful to notice that both hands stay in the same five-finger position throughout, so you won't need to move.

BLACK MAGIC

SOLO

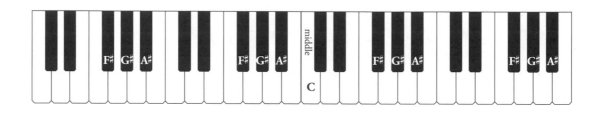

Fairly Slow

PERFORMANCE NOTES

This piece is intended to be learned by rote. This means your teacher will tell you the notes to play and you will then memorize the note patterns without music, as if by magic!

RHYTHM FOCUS

Of course, we know that no music is really committed to memory by magic. To help you learn this music, tap out the rhythm of the piece below before you move on to the note patterns. You'll need both hands; the right hand will tap the treble-clef rhythm and the left hand will tap the bass-clef rhythm.

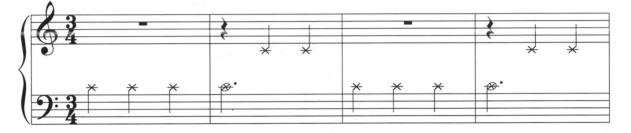

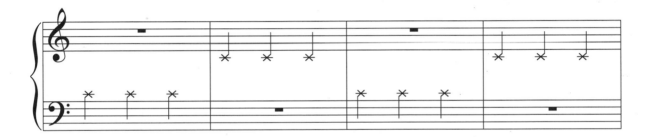

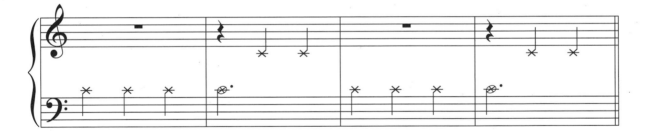

NOTE FOCUS

All the notes in this piece are played on black keys, so try to keep your hands placed over the note patterns, guiding the fingers into place. Black keys are smaller and narrower than white keys, which is why we need to move the relevant finger forward in plenty of time, hovering over the black key.

The music in measures 5–9 moves up and down the keyboard in a set pattern. If you are able to, try adding the right sustaining pedal by depressing your foot for the entire passage. Otherwise, ask your teacher to do it. Enjoy the sound!

No dynamics or sound indications have been added. So, have fun adding your own. Be creative and use your imagination to make your performance as magical as possible.

THE MERRY CLOWN

DUET

PERFORMANCE NOTES

This is a duet that you can play with a friend or with your teacher. Have fun as our happy clown trips up and down the keyboard.

RHYTHM FOCUS

Duets must be played as a team. Getting the eighth notes perfectly together in this piece will take careful practice. Try tapping through the music, saying the beat count "1–and–2–and–3–and." Have a practice on this short passage, first.

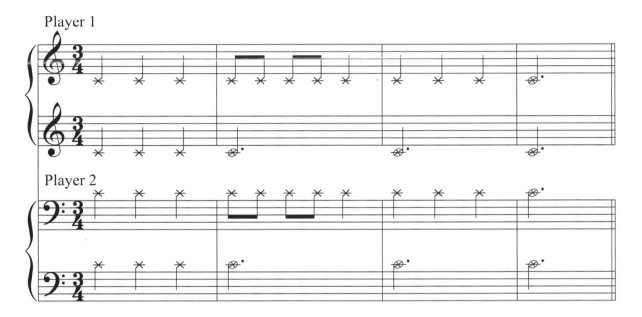

NOTE FOCUS

This piece gets gradually louder and louder. Dynamics are another important aspect to practice with your duet partner. Try matching each other's dynamics in this short exercise.

When you perform this piece, "Player 2" will play their left hand an octave lower than written. This is shown by the 8vb – – – – – – – – – – – – – – – – sign on the music.

A SNAKE IN THE GARDEN

SOLO WITH TEACHER ACCOMPANIMENT

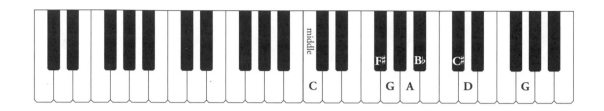

PERFORMANCE NOTES

Finding a snake in your garden doesn't happen every day. There are lots of unusual and interesting sounds in this piece created by the sharp (♯) and flat (♭) signs in front of the notes. Be careful that you don't get bitten!

NOTE FOCUS

At the very beginning and end of this piece, you are playing the melody while your teacher accompanies. Keep your fingertips hovering over the black keys. Your left hand stays in the same hand position throughout. Your right hand changes position in measures 5–6, where you accompany your teacher who now plays the tune. Make sure everyone can hear your teacher's tune in these measures!

Find all the different notes that have flats or sharps in front of them and write them on the staff below as noteheads without stems. The first one has been done for you.

ACCOMPANIMENT

BELLS

SOLO WITH TEACHER ACCOMPANIMENT

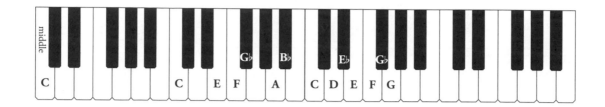

PERFORMANCE NOTES

Majestic bells ring out for all to hear. In this piece, your teacher will play the accompaniment, which consists of rolling chords. Your solo part must "ring" out above it, just like bells. There are two half notes in every measure. Both of these can be played with your third finger, firstly in the left hand and then in the right-hand part.

NOTE FOCUS

There is an accent symbol (>) above each note, so be sure to give lots of sound. All the notes must be bold and powerful, and are to be caught in the sustaining pedal. This will provide a wonderful resonance, just like bells.

Don't forget to play your solo part an octave higher, as indicated by the 8va - - - - - - - sign above the staff.

Why don't you experiment by *improvising* bell sounds on your piano or keyboard? Improvising means to make music up from your imagination. If you can't reach the pedals, ask your teacher to depress the right sustaining pedal while you play bright, bold notes or groups of notes, just like bells ringing out.

ACCOMPANIMENT

ROLLING WAVES

SOLO WITH TEACHER ACCOMPANIMENT

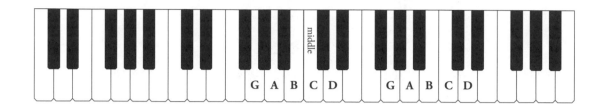

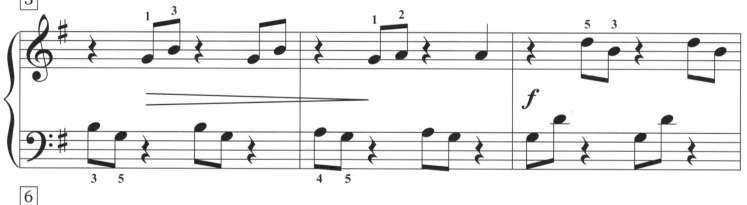

PERFORMANCE NOTES

There are almost continuous eighth notes in this piece, just like the continuous rolling of waves on the shore.

RHYTHM FOCUS

Your right and left hands don't quite play together here, which can make things a little tricky. If you need help, try tapping out the rhythm using the notation below. You can also say the beat count while you tap: "1–and–2–and–3–and–4–and."

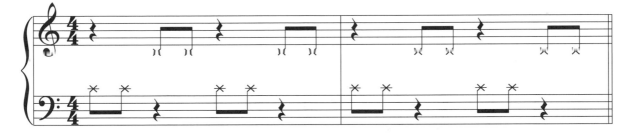

NOTE FOCUS

Try warming up for this piece by playing a five-finger G major scale, like the one below.

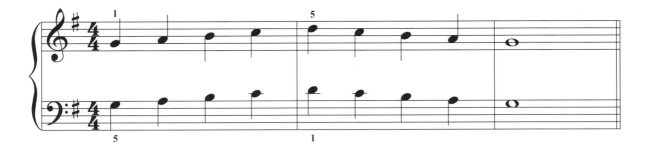

A smooth (*legato*) touch is needed. Each note should be connected to the next without any gaps in the sound. If your teacher uses the sustaining (right) pedal in each measure, there will be a lovely echo effect.

ACCOMPANIMENT

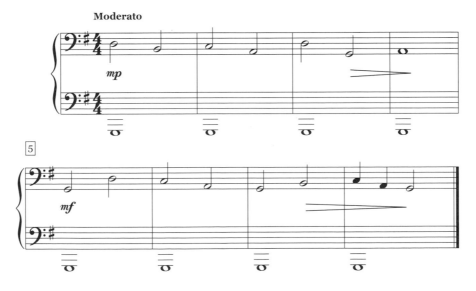

SUGARY DOUGHNUT

SOLO

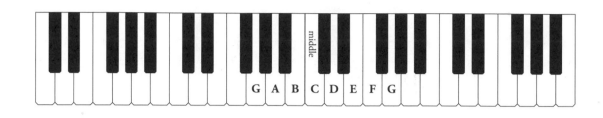

Fast and Bold

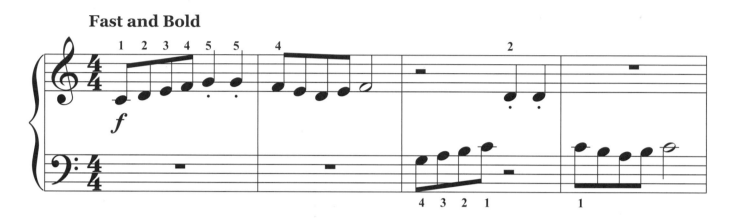

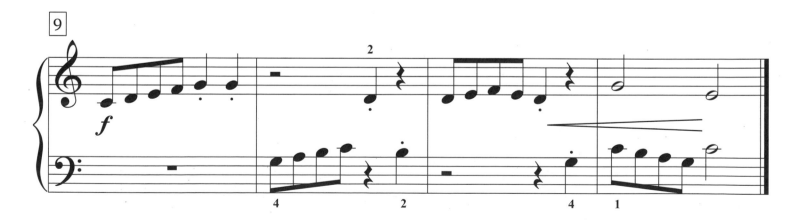

PERFORMANCE NOTES

Sweet and gooey, doughnuts are such a treat. Rather like this little piano piece!

RHYTHM FOCUS

Each of your five fingers can fly in this piece because it is fast! You might like to practice at a slower tempo, gradually increasing the speed as you become more confident. Whatever speed you are practicing, it's important to maintain a strict beat count: "1–and–2–and–3–and–4–and." The "ands" will ensure that you don't speed up or slow down during a performance.

NOTE FOCUS

Keep eighth-note patterns very smooth, with each note joined to the next without any gaps in sound. Notice that some of the quarter notes have dots underneath or above the noteheads. These notes are to be played *staccato* (very short and detached), so try to leave them quickly, as if the keys are hot. Whole and half notes must be held for their full value.

Hands should ideally be hovering over the notes ready to play, especially at measures 3 and 10, where notes are passed swiftly between left and right.

This five-finger C major scale will be very useful. Practice it at various speeds, keeping your beat count consistent. You could also play the pattern with varying touches (or *articulation*). Start with smooth notes and no gaps. Then again, with short, detatched notes.

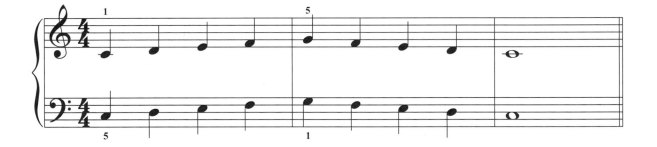

KICK THE CAN

SOLO WITH TEACHER ACCOMPANIMENT

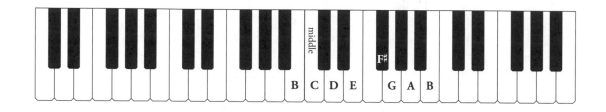

PERFORMANCE NOTES

"Kick the can" is a great game to play. Your right and left hands chase each other all over the keyboard in this piece full of eighth notes.

RHYTHM FOCUS

To learn the rhythm correctly, tap out your part on your knee or the piano lid. Your teacher could tap the accompaniment part with you, too. Practice the following exercise in order to learn this important rhythmic pattern.

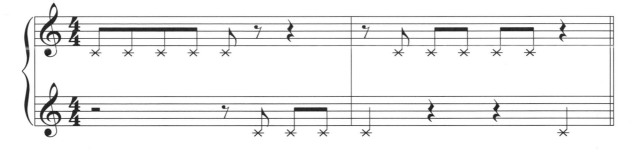

NOTE FOCUS

When a note moves above or below the five lines of the staff, we place the notehead on a short line. This is called a *ledger line*. In this piece, the note B (a half step below middle C) is on a ledger line. Practice writing some Bs on the treble staff below. Then, find and circle them in the music.

The *dynamics* (louds and softs) are important in this piece, beginning at *mezzo-forte* (moderately loud) with a *crescendo* (getting louder) to measure 4. From measure 5, a *forte* (or loud) sound is necessary. Then, together with your teacher, crescendo to the final measure, which needs a really powerful tone.

ACCOMPANIMENT

HOT-AIR BALLOON

SOLO WITH TEACHER ACCOMPANIMENT

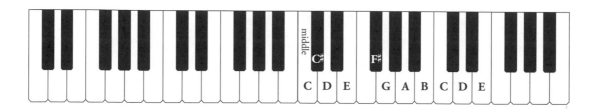

PERFORMANCE NOTES

You're about to go on a beautiful journey, moving between several different hand positions in your hot-air balloon.

RHYTHM FOCUS

It will be very important to play all your eighth notes with a smooth and even sound. We don't want a bumpy balloon ride! Why not try tapping this extract from the piece, saying the beat count "1–and–2–and–3–and–4–and" (counting eighth notes)?

ACCOMPANIMENT

BAROQUE CAPERS

SOLO

PERFORMANCE NOTES

This piece is written in a style of western European music from around 400 years ago, during what we call the Baroque period. Keyboard music at this time was often played on an instrument called a harpsichord. The harpsichord has a different sound from that of the piano because its strings are plucked with a quill, whereas those on the piano are struck with a soft-felt hammer. Maybe you are playing this piece on a keyboard that has a harpsichord sound? Try it out for fun!

RHYTHM FOCUS

You might like to practice the rhythm of this piece using separate hands, saying an eighth note beat count: "1–and–2–and–3–and–4–and." Here's an extract to be worked on in this way.

First, the right hand.

Then, the left hand.

And finally, putting them both together. Remember, your right hand will tap the rhythm in the treble clef. Your left hand will tap the rhythm in the bass clef.

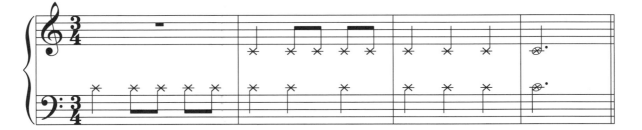

NOTE FOCUS

When a note goes higher or lower than the staff, we use small lines on the notehead. These lines are called *ledger lines*. Here are the notes with ledger lines used in this piece as noteheads without stems. Write each letter name underneath the staff. Then, locate where these notes are in the music and on the keyboard using the keyboard diagram.

YE OLDE CASTLE

DUET

PERFORMANCE NOTES

This is a duet for you and a friend. The combination of notes in this piece makes us imagine a time long ago of knights and castles. The music uses what is called the "D natural minor scale." Why not ask your teacher about this scale?

RHYTHM FOCUS

Let's play tic-tac-toe! Ask your duet partner to play with you using half notes (the 0s), and you can play using eighth notes (the Xs). Place the eighth notes in a row of three before your partner places their half notes and you have won the game!

NOTE FOCUS

"Andante" means to play at a "walking pace," so be sure not to play too fast. A smooth touch and a warm sound are important. Try to follow the *crescendo* and *decrescendo* markings, too. Imagine a huge castle, home to brave knights and a royal family.

Play the D natural minor five-finger scale, which will help you become accustomed to the sound of this piece. If you play one hand each, you'll be able to work on playing beautifully together, too.

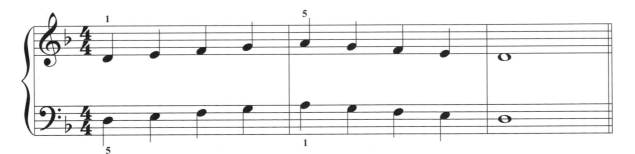

SQUIRRELS ON THE FENCE

SOLO

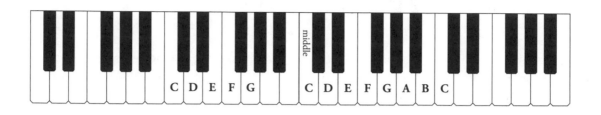

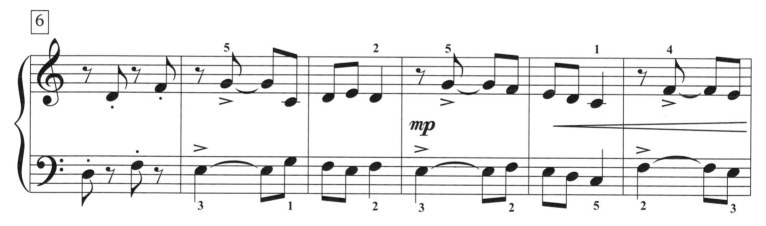

PERFORMANCE NOTES

Squirrels love to jump from fence to fence! This piece features two little squirrels, one in the left-hand part and another in the right-hand part. They are busy fence-hopping.

RHYTHM FOCUS

There are two quarter-note beats to every measure in this piece. Measures 1–2, 5–6, and 13–14 need to be played with a *staccato* touch, which means short and detached. Leave each eighth note quickly but during practice say the beat count "1–and–2–and." Counting eighth notes in this way will ensure that you don't rush ahead.

NOTE FOCUS

The squirrels are darting around and chatting to one another. Aim to put more emphasis on the notes with accents (>).

In measures 16–17, you will notice a wavy line between the two half notes. This is called a *glissando*. To play it, turn your left hand so the palm is facing upwards and place the back of your fingers (balancing on your fingernails) over the notes. Then, depress the keys and slide over the white keys, from top C to bottom C.

Land firmly on the low C, with the third finger of your right hand moving over the left hand. If you do this at speed, it will sound like squirrels falling off the fence!

DOLLY DAYDREAM

SOLO

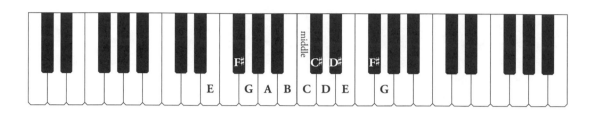

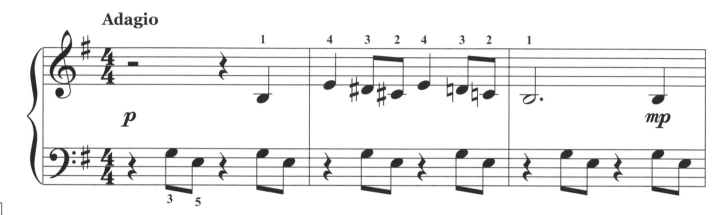

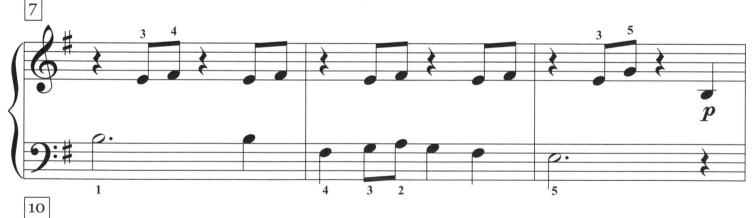

PERFORMANCE NOTES

This piece feels quite sad. Think about what Dolly might be sad about as you get to know the music. Using your imagination can help bring a piece of music to life.

RHYTHM FOCUS

Let's play tic-tac-toe! Ask your teacher to play with you using quarter notes (the 0s), and you can play using eighth notes (the Xs). Place the eighth notes in a row of three before your teacher places their quarter notes and you have won the game! To help, an eighth note has already been added.

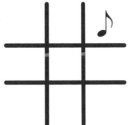

NOTE FOCUS

This piece uses the notes of a scale called "E melodic minor." The notes for a five-finger E minor scale are written below. Practice playing this at a slow tempo ("Adagio") and with a smooth sound, creating a sad atmosphere.

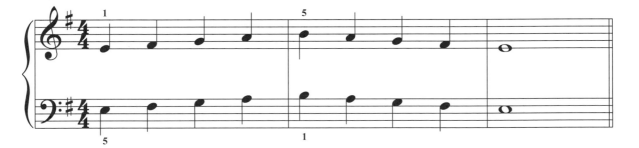

"Dolly Daydream" use the black keys F♯, C♯, and D♯. Be sure to play these black keys firmly with the tips of your fingers. Sometimes, you will need to play the C and D white keys immediately after the black C♯ and D♯ keys. This is where your imagination comes in because the music sounds so sad. Play these moments with a beautiful, smooth touch and lots of expression for a moving performance.

45

SPEEDING ALONG

SOLO

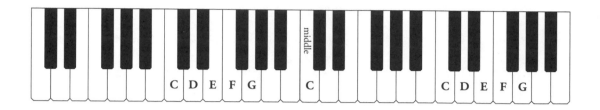

PERFORMANCE NOTES

This is such a fun piece to play and it speeds along at quite a pace. Hold on to your hats!

RHYTHM FOCUS

This piece uses a dotted rhythmic pattern on several occasions. Notice the beat count needed to make sure the rhythm is played accurately. Try clapping and counting along to this rhythm, which will help you when you come to perform the music.

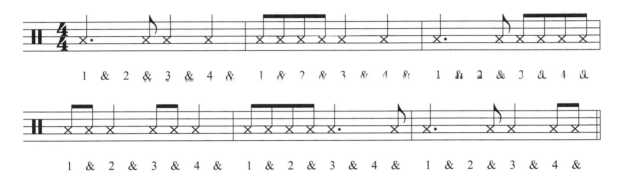

NOTE FOCUS

"Speeding Along" contains three-note chords in the left hand. These chords change in every measure, so practice hands separately to be confident with the note patterns. The hand position stays the same throughout, which will give you time to prepare each new pattern.

This left-hand exercise will help you to get this just right. Work on it at a speed you are comfortable with.

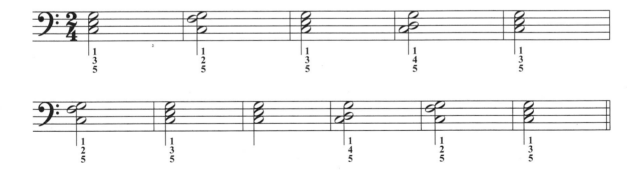

TANGO-TASTIC

SOLO

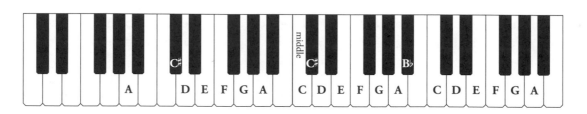

Con moto

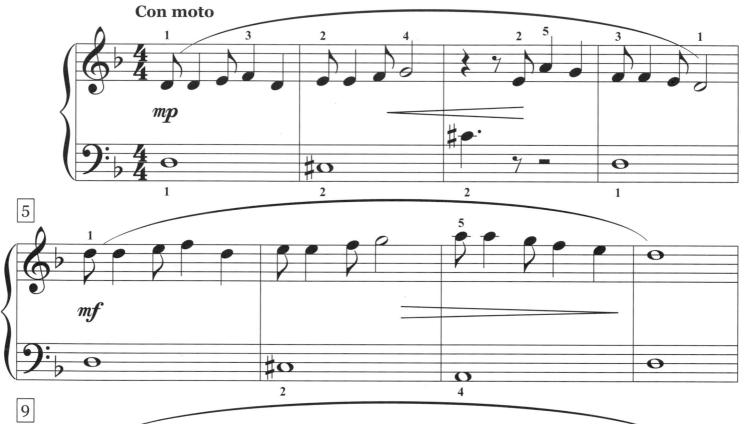

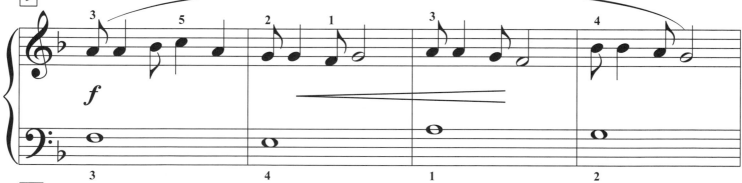

PERFORMANCE NOTES

A tango is a dance that comes from Argentina, a country in South America. This dance is intended for two people and it has energy and passion. It can often be quite sad in character, too.

RHYTHM FOCUS

Rhythm is very important in all dances but especially in the tango. Your right-hand part contains the melody, which has a fantastic but quite tricky rhythm that is important for the character of the dance. You might want to practice it separately for security, saying the beat count steadily.

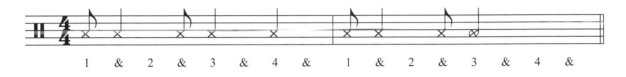

1 & 2 & 3 & 4 & 1 & 2 & 3 & 4 &

NOTE FOCUS

The two eighth notes in the right-hand part of measure 1 (beats 1 and 2) should be played lightly, with greater emphasis on the first quarter note (D). This emphasis should be observed throughout.

There are hand-position changes in the right-hand part at measures 5, 9, and 13. The left hand will also need to change position at measures 3, 4, 9, and 13 so it's a good idea to practice each hand separately to gain confidence.

EARLY BLUES

SOLO

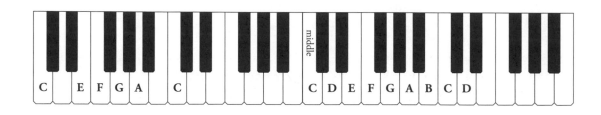

PERFORMANCE NOTES

This piece is based on the style of music known as "blues." Blues music originated in West Africa and became established in the United States of America over 100 years ago.

RHYTHM FOCUS

Your left hand keeps a simple quarter-note beat. So, it's the right hand that needs most of the rhythmic focus. Practice tapping the right hand separately, saying the beat count if you wish ("1–and–2–and–3–and–4–and"). Here are the two important rhythmic ideas in the music.

NOTE FOCUS

The accent marks (>) play a vital role in the groove of this piece, so be sure to play them powerfully when they appear.

The right-hand part romps around the keyboard. As this piece is fast ("Presto"), you'll need to be prepared to move swiftly. Begin by practicing it slowly, gradually building up to performance speed as you grow in security and confidence.

A BICYCLE RIDE FOR TWO

PERFORMANCE NOTES

This is a musical ride for two! Perform it with a fellow student, friend, or teacher.

RHYTHM FOCUS

Tap out the rhythm of this piece on the piano lid or your knees to work on playing together perfectly. You could start by both tapping the rhythm below, which occurs many times in the piece. Say the beat count together if that helps, too ("1, 2, 3, 4").

NOTE FOCUS

The right hand for both players contains the melody and the left-hand parts accompany. Aim to practice the two right-hand musical lines together without the left hands.

A smooth *legato* touch should capture the joy and fun of riding along together. "Player 1's" right-hand part is played an octave higher than written; this is indicated by the 8va ------- sign.

Try to make sure that you both *crescendo* (get louder) at the same moment from measures 10–13. The ending should be loud! Try playing this exercise together to match each other's dynamics.

Also available in the series...

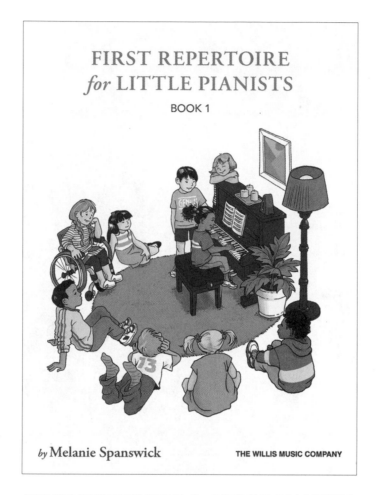

FIRST REPERTOIRE *for* **LITTLE PIANISTS**

BOOK 1

HL00385204

Available at all good music stores.